GERM INVADERS
TAKING ON COLDS

MEGAN BORGERT-SPANIOL

Big Buddy Books

An Imprint of Abdo Publishing
abdobooks.com

abdobooks.com

Published by Abdo Publishing, a division of ABDO, PO Box 398166, Minneapolis, Minnesota 55439. Copyright © 2021 by Abdo Consulting Group, Inc. International copyrights reserved in all countries. No part of this book may be reproduced in any form without written permission from the publisher. Big Buddy Books™ is a trademark and logo of Abdo Publishing.

Printed in the United States of America, North Mankato, Minnesota
102020
012021

Design: Sarah DeYoung, Mighty Media, Inc.
Production: Mighty Media, Inc.
Editor: Rebecca Felix

Cover Photographs: David S. Goodsell, RCSB Protein Data Bank/Wellcome Collection (rhinovirus); Shutterstock (fist)
Interior Photographs: Shutterstock (all)
Design Elements: Shutterstock (all)

Library of Congress Control Number: 2020940281

Publisher's Cataloging-in-Publication Data
Names: Borgert-Spaniol, Megan, author.
Title: Taking on colds / by Megan Borgert-Spaniol
Description: Minneapolis, Minnesota : Abdo Publishing, 2021 | Series: Germ invaders | Includes online resources and index
Identifiers: ISBN 9781532194245 (lib. bdg.) | ISBN 9781098213602 (ebook)
Subjects: LCSH: Cold (Disease)--Juvenile literature. | Cold prevention (Medicine)--Juvenile literature. | Cold (Disease)--Prevention--Juvenile literature. | Health behavior--Juvenile literature. | Immunology--Juvenile literature. | Hygiene--Juvenile literature.
Classification: DDC 616.079--dc23

CONTENTS

Your Amazing Body 4
When a Cold Attacks 6
All about Colds 8
Catching a Cold 10
Your Immune System 12
Cold Season 14
Do You Have a Cold? 16
Cold vs. Flu 18
No Vaccine 20
Getting Better 22
When to See a Doctor 24
Cold Complications 26
Healthy Habits 28
Glossary 30
Online Resources 31
Index 32

YOUR AMAZING BODY

You are amazing! So is your body. Most of the time your body works just fine. But sometimes germs **invade** it. Germs can make you sick. One common illness is the cold. Most people get sick with a cold at least once a year.

GET TO KNOW GERMS

Germs are tiny **organisms**. They can live inside people, plants, and animals. There are four main types of germs.

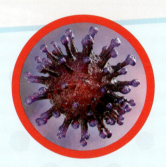

VIRUSES

Viruses are parasitic. This means they cannot survive on their own. They require a host cell to reproduce. Colds are caused by viruses.

BACTERIA

Bacteria are single-celled creatures. They can survive on their own or inside another living organism.

PROTOZOA

Protozoa are single-celled creatures. Some can survive on their own. Others are parasitic.

FUNGI

Fungi are plant-like organisms. They get their food from people, plants, and animals.

WHEN A COLD ATTACKS

A cold virus attacks your body one or two days before you start feeling **symptoms**. It usually takes about one week for your body to fight the virus.

CONTACT

A person with a cold coughs, sneezes, or talks near you. Their germs enter the air.

INVASION

The cold virus germs enter your mouth, nose, or tear ducts.

ATTACK

The cold virus attaches to the lining of your nose, throat, or tear ducts. The virus begins to make copies. It spreads throughout your upper **respiratory system**.

ALARM

After about two days, your immune system notices the virus. Your body sends white blood cells to fight the virus.

FIGHT

Your body produces more **mucus** than normal to trap the germs and send them out through coughing or a runny nose. You may also get a fever. This rise in body temperature helps kill the virus.

RECOVER

After one or two weeks, your white blood cells have destroyed the virus. You start to feel better!

ALL ABOUT COLDS

A cold is an **infection** of the upper **respiratory system**. This system includes the nose, throat, and **sinuses**.

There are more than 200 types of cold viruses. The most common type is called a **rhinovirus**.

Because there are so many cold viruses, colds are the most common infectious illnesses in the United States. Colds are especially common among kids. Kids can get eight or more colds each year!

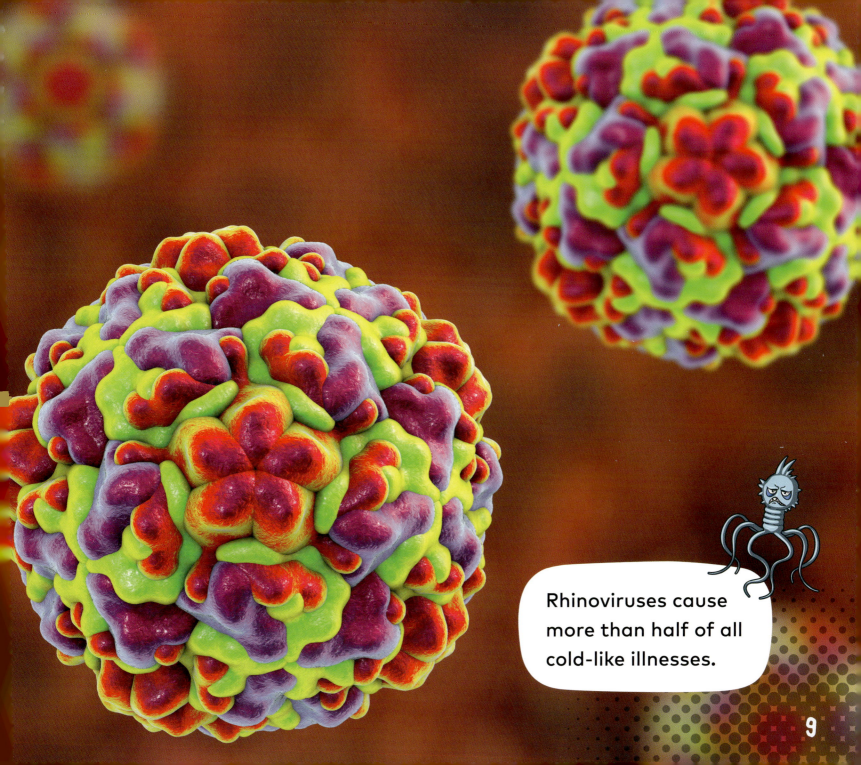

Rhinoviruses cause more than half of all cold-like illnesses.

CATCHING A COLD

Cold viruses can spread in a few ways. One is through direct contact, such as shaking hands with a person who has a cold.

You might also touch an object a sick person recently touched, such as a doorknob. If you touch a person's germs and then touch your eyes, nose, or mouth, you might catch their cold.

Cold viruses also spread through the air. When a sick person coughs, sneezes, or talks, tiny virus droplets travel through the air. If you are nearby, you might breathe them in and catch the cold.

A cold virus can travel up to 12 feet (3.7 m) through the air when a sick person coughs or sneezes!

YOUR IMMUNE SYSTEM

When you catch a cold, your immune system goes into action. This is your body's system that fights back against **infections**.

White blood cells do a lot of work for the immune system. They attack and destroy **invading** viruses. They also make antibodies. These are special **proteins**. They stay in your body after a virus is gone. If the same virus comes back, the antibodies attack it.

Every time you fight a new virus, your immune system gets stronger. Your body becomes better prepared to fight that virus again. Because of this, kids get fewer colds as they get older.

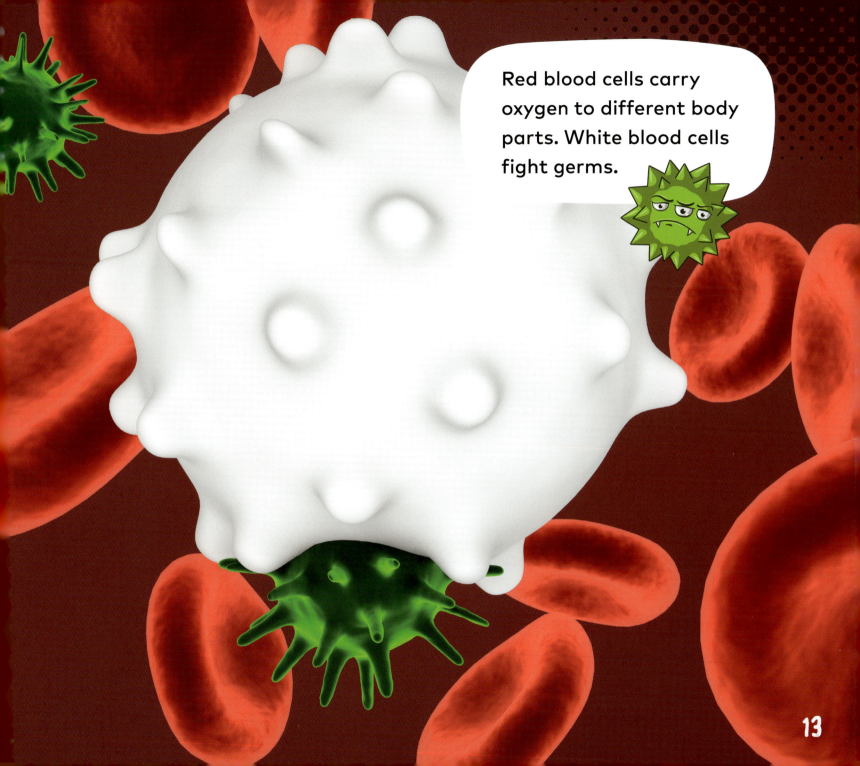

COLD SEASON

In the United States, most colds occur between September and March. Scientists think this may be because kids are in school during these months. Students are physically close at school, allowing germs to easily spread.

Cold weather can also help colds spread. People spend more time indoors during colder months. This brings people into closer contact, making it easier for germs to spread. Research also suggests viruses spread more easily in cold, dry air than in warm, moist air.

Experts say colds cause US students to miss a total of 22 million school days each year.

DO YOU HAVE A COLD?

Cold **symptoms** usually appear two or three days after **infection**. These symptoms often include a sore throat and stuffy nose. You might be coughing or sneezing. You could also have a headache or a low fever.

You are most **contagious** in the first few days after symptoms begin. So, it's a good idea to stay home when you have a cold. This will help prevent spreading the virus to others.

Many cold symptoms result from the extra mucus your body creates to help fight the virus.

COLD VS. FLU

Some people think they have a cold when they really have influenza, or the flu. The flu is another common illness caused by viruses. Flu **symptoms** can be similar to cold symptoms. However, flu symptoms are usually worse than cold symptoms.

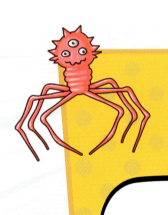

FLU OR COLD?

These illnesses share many symptoms. But some symptoms are more common of the flu.

BOTH
- Sore Throat
- Runny Nose
- Tiredness
- Cough
- Sneezing

FLU
- Fever
- Chills and Sweats
- Extreme Exhaustion

It can be hard to tell the difference between a cold and the flu. Doctors can do tests to find out for sure.

19

NO VACCINE

One big difference between the cold and the flu involves **vaccines**. People can get a vaccination each year to protect them against the flu. However, there are no cold vaccines.

One reason for this is the great number of cold viruses. A cold vaccine would have to target each of the more than 200 types. So far, scientists have struggled to do this. But they continue working to create a cold vaccine.

SCIENCE BREAKTHROUGH

Scientists first discovered **rhinoviruses** in the 1950s. They continued discovering different types of rhinovirus through the 1990s.

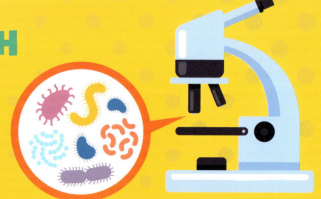

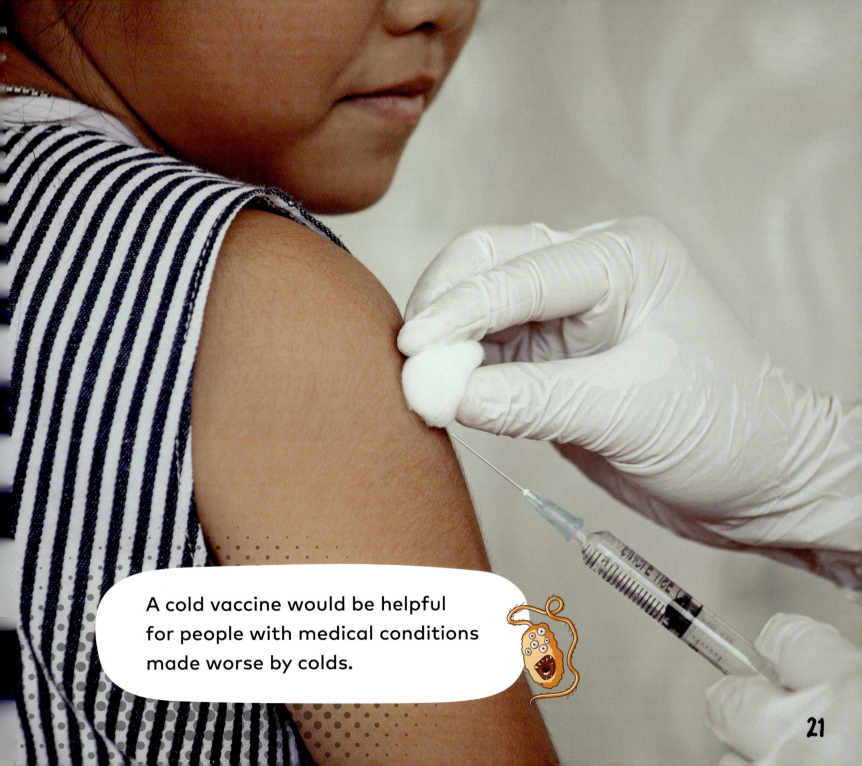

A cold vaccine would be helpful for people with medical conditions made worse by colds.

21

GETTING BETTER

Cold **symptoms** usually last seven to ten days. During this time, you can help ease your symptoms a few ways.

Get lots of rest. Rest lets your body use its energy to fight the virus. Drink lots of water too. This helps thin the **mucus** in your nose and lungs.

While you recover, you can also use natural **remedies** to help ease your symptoms. Many **over-the-counter** medicines can make you feel better too.

22

MEDICINES

COUGH EXPECTORANT
Helps the body cough up **mucus**

NASAL DECONGESTANT
Unclogs a stuffed nose

PAIN RELIEVER
Relieves fever and sore throat pain

THROAT LOZENGES AND SPRAYS
Relieve sore throat pain

NATURAL REMEDIES

SALT WATER
Gargling with salt water soothes a sore throat

WARM LIQUID
Helps mucus flow from your body and soothes a sore throat

VITAMIN C
May help improve cold **symptoms** if taken regularly before getting sick

WHEN TO SEE A DOCTOR

Most people battle cold **symptoms** with rest, medicine, and natural **remedies**. But sometimes symptoms are harmful. In these cases, you might be dealing with more than a cold.

If you experience **severe** symptoms, call your doctor. Also call your doctor if symptoms don't begin to improve within ten days. The doctor can make sure you are not sick with a more serious illness.

If your symptoms feel serious, tell an adult.

COLD COMPLICATIONS

Most of the time, colds go away after about a week. But sometimes colds lead to more serious issues. If you show signs of these **complications**, go to the doctor right away.

SINUS INFECTION

This causes pressure around the eyes, cheeks, and forehead. Other **symptoms** may include fever and a yellow-green nasal **mucus**.

EAR INFECTION

Ear **infections** cause pressure or pain in one or both ears. Fluid may drain from an infected ear.

BRONCHITIS

This happens when the tubes leading to the lungs become swollen and produce a lot of **mucus**. Mucus buildup in the lungs and coughing up mucus are signs of bronchitis.

PNEUMONIA

Pneumonia causes air sacs in the lungs to fill with fluid. It often causes chest pain, coughing, fever, and difficulty breathing.

27

HEALTHY HABITS

By practicing some healthy habits, you can help protect yourself from getting or spreading cold viruses.

- ☐ Wash your hands often for at least 20 seconds with soap and water.
- ☐ Avoid sharing dishes with sick people.
- ☐ Get plenty of sleep.
- ☐ Drink lots of water.
- ☐ Cough and sneeze into tissues or your elbow.

Even with healthy habits, you might still catch a cold. But thanks to your amazing immune system, science, and some healthy habits, your body is ready to face these germ **invaders**!

GLOSSARY

complication—a second condition that develops during the course of a primary disease or condition.

contagious—having a disease you can easily spread to others by direct or indirect contact.

infect—to enter and cause disease in. Something or someone with a disease is infected, and the condition is called an infection. Something that causes an infection is infectious.

invade—to enter and spread with the intent to take over. Something that does this is an invader.

mucus (MYOO-kuhs)—thick, slippery, protective fluid from the body.

organism—a living thing.

over-the-counter—available to purchase at stores without a doctor's prescription.

protein (PROH-teen)—a combination of certain kinds of chemical elements found in all plant and animal cells.

remedy—a food, medicine, or treatment that treats or relieves a disease or its symptoms.

respiratory system—a system of organs including the nose, nasal passages, pharynx, larynx, trachea, bronchi, and lungs, which together function to allow breathing.

rhinovirus—any one of a family of picornaviruses that cause respiratory infections in humans.

severe (suh-VIHR)—causing danger, hardship, or pain.

sinus—a narrow, hollow tract in the skull that connects with the nostrils.

symptom—a noticeable change in the normal working of the body. A symptom indicates or accompanies disease, sickness, or other malfunction.

vaccine (vak-SEEN)—a substance given through a shot to prevent illness or disease. Receiving this shot is called vaccination.

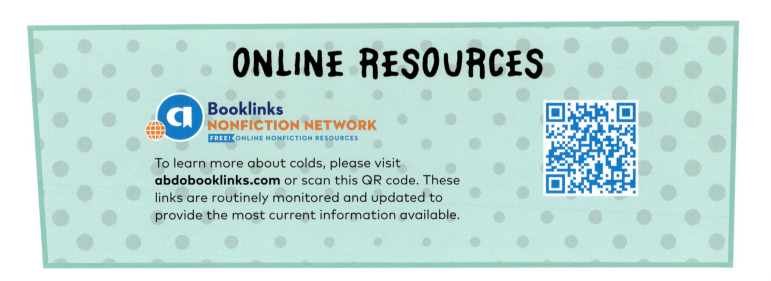

ONLINE RESOURCES

Booklinks
NONFICTION NETWORK
FREE! ONLINE NONFICTION RESOURCES

To learn more about colds, please visit abdobooklinks.com or scan this QR code. These links are routinely monitored and updated to provide the most current information available.

INDEX

animals, 5
antibodies, 12

bacteria, 5
bronchitis, 27

coughing, 6, 7, 10, 16, 18, 23, 27, 28

doctors, 19, 24, 26

ear infection, 26
eyes, 6, 10, 26

fever, 7, 16, 18, 23, 26, 27
flu. *See* influenza
fungi, 5

headache, 16

immune system, 7, 12, 28
influenza, 18, 19, 20
invasion, 4, 6, 12, 28

lungs, 22, 27

mucus, 7, 16, 22, 23, 26, 27

nose, 6, 7, 8, 10, 16, 18, 22, 23, 26

over-the-counter medicines, 22, 23, 24

plants, 5
pneumonia, 27
protozoa, 5

red blood cells, 13
remedies, 22, 23, 24
respiratory system, 7, 8
rhinoviruses, 8, 9, 20

scientists, 14, 20
sinuses, 8, 26
sneezing, 6, 10, 16, 18, 28
spreading, 6, 7, 10, 14, 16, 28
symptoms, 6, 7, 10, 16, 18, 22, 23, 24, 25, 26, 27, 28

throat, 7, 8, 16, 18, 23

vaccines, 20, 21

washing hands, 28
white blood cells, 7, 12, 13